Judith Blacklock's Flower recipes for
AUTUMN

The Flower Press

Published by
The Flower Press Ltd
3 East Avenue
Bournemouth
BH3 7BW

Text Copyright © Judith Blacklock, 2008

This first edition published 2008

A CIP catalogue record for this book is available from the British Library.

ISBN 13: 978 0 9552391 4 4

Design: Amanda Hawkes

Printed and bound in China by C & C Offset Printing Co., Ltd.

Contents

Introduction

For the flower designer autumn is the season of abundance, of flowers, cones, berries, fruits and leaves. The garden, the hedgerows and the flower shops are full of strong rich colour from the stunning pinks of the nerines, the gold of *Solidago*, the orange of Chinese lanterns, the red of the berries together with the changing colour of autumn foliage – green through to red, gold and brown.

Vegetables, cones, nuts and fruits can be added to the flowers to give strong bold colour, form and texture. Easily obtainable, they can complement the flowers and give added interest inexpensively.

This book is the fourth in my recipe series and contains 49 simple and accessible designs. All are easy to create and if you do not have a particular ingredient the advice and steps should mean that you have no problem finding an alternative. Giving inspiration is one of the most satisfying ways of teaching and I hope that for the more experienced a few of these designs may spark your creativity.

Judith

Hydrangea heights

A tall cylindrical container offers a great opportunity to be inventive.

Method

1 Add a little water to the container.

2 Cut the first *Hydrangea* to half the height of the container and the second equal to the height. Remove most or all of the leaves.

3 Put the shorter flower in the container and then insert the stem of the longer one down through the petals of the first.

You will need

· cylindrical container – this one is 40 cm (16 in) tall
· 2 *Hydrangea*

Design tips

The taller your container, the more flowers you can use. Cylindrical containers are widely available in a variety of sizes but make sure it is not too wide or the hydrangeas will not stay upright.

You can wind aluminium wire around the stems of the *Hydrangea* if you wish to decorate them further.

Take care when handling large glass containers and always pick up from the base rather than the rim.

You will need

- autumnal coloured container with a wide opening – this one is 15 cm (6 in) tall and 20 cm (8 in) wide
- birch twigs and dried leaves from the woods or the garden
- 5-7 *Chrysanthemum*
- 5-7 roses such as the brown rose *Rosa* 'Leonidas'

Design tip

This monochromatic colour scheme is evocative of autumn but try adding deep purple, red or pink flowers to the design to change the mood completely.

A woodland walk can yield all sorts of interesting plant material in the autumn such as twigs, cones, chestnuts and leaves in an array of wonderful colours.

Method

1 Mass the twigs together in the container. They will support all the other stems so there is no need for foam. Pour in a little water.

2 Add the dried leaves – their ends do not need to be in water.

3 Add the other plant material to the container, placing the stems between the twigs so that the flower heads are evident.

Pina colada

Baby pineapples are fun to use in flower arranging. They add wonderful colour, texture and novelty.

You will need

- container about 15 cm (6 in) tall
- floral foam
- 3 mini pineapples (*Ananas*)
- small apples (*Malus*)
- cocktail sticks
- 5-7 red roses
- 4-5 stems red *Hypericum*
- *Galax* or ivy leaves
- berried ivy (*Hedera*)

Design tips

Galax leaves are very useful to have around – they have a smooth texture and a strong stem. When purchased, soak them underwater for 10 minutes, and then shake off excess water. Store them in a plastic bag in the vegetable compartment of the fridge and they will keep for weeks.

Medium to large single ivy leaves are a good alternative to the *Galax* in this design.

Method

1 Secure the foam in the container so that it rises above the rim.

2 If the mini pineapples do not have a stem, insert cocktail sticks firmly into each of their bases. Position them in the foam at regular intervals.

3 Repeat with the apples. This will establish a basic shape.

4 Reinforce the shape with the roses and *Hypericum*.

5 Fill in any gaps with the *Galax* or ivy leaves together with the berried ivy.

Poppy power

Stylish and utterly simple, this is a quick and easy design that will last throughout the season.

You will need

- 3 lily vases at varying heights – two are 60 cm (24 in) tall and one is 40 cm (16 in) tall
- 14-15 poppy seedheads, fresh or dried
- decorative wire
- 1 stem *Hypericum*

Design tips

To dry poppy seedheads hang them in a bunch upside-down. Place a paper bag over the heads to catch the seeds as they disperse.

If you are using fresh seedheads they have a tendency to go mouldy so do keep an eye on them.

Method

1 For each vase, take 4-5 poppy seedheads and place them on the table in front of you. The longest should rise just above the rim of the container so cut this one to size and place it with the end of its stem on the edge of the table. Place each poppy in turn so that it is one head shorter than the previous. Cut the stem ends that hang over the edge of the table.

2 Place the seedheads in each of the vases.

3 Remove the *Hypericum* berries from the stem with their calyx still attached. Thread them onto lengths of decorative wire and attach these around the base of each container.

Good enough to eat

A sumptuous design for the table that incorporates the latest trend of using fruit and vegetables with flowers.

Method

1 Check that your container is waterproof. If it is not, then line it with a section of black plastic bin liner.

2 Place a piece of un-soaked foam in the bottom of the container. This should rise no more than half way up the inside.

3 Insert the candles into the foam along the length of the container. (For extra security see Techniques pages 94–95).

4 Pile your peppers into the container but leave space for the roses.

5 Fill the orchid tubes with water and insert a rose in each tube.

6 Add the flowers to the design.

You will need

- oval container – this one is 15 cm (6 in) tall and 20 cm (8 in) wide
- black plastic bin liner
- floral foam
- 7 slender candles or 3 fatter candles
- 15-20 mini peppers in an assortment of colours
- 5 plastic orchid tubes
- 5 red roses

Pumpkin panoply

Pumpkins are redolent of witches, lanterns and Halloween. Their strong bold form, colour and texture work harmoniously with flowers from the autumn garden.

You will need

· **pumpkin – about 23 cm (9 in) in diameter at widest point**
· **sharp thin flexible knife**
· **bowl to fit inside the pumpkin**
· **floral foam**
· **3 bloom *Chrysanthemum***
· **4 yellow roses**
· **3 red roses**
· **3 pincushion protea (*Leucospermum*)**
· **1 stem of Chinese lantern (*Physalis*)**
· **rosehips**
· **3 *Aspidistra* leaves**
· **Boston ivy (*Parthenocissus tricuspidata*) or large ivy leaves**
· **decorative wire**
· **beads**

Method

1   Carve out the pumpkin with the knife. Remove as much flesh as possible as this deteriorates rapidly.

2   Place the bowl in the cavity. Cut foam to rise about 2.5 cm (1 in) above the rim. Soak the foam and place it in the bowl.

3   Cut the flowers short and insert in groups over the foam together with the fruits.

4   Tuck the Boston ivy leaves under the flowers so that they are framed by the foliage.

5   To fill in any gaps roll the *Aspidistra* leaves. Use a tiny amount of fix to keep the roll in place.

6   Thread beads onto the decorative wire. Twist the wire around the bead after each addition.

7   Wrap the wired beads around the *Aspidistra* leaves and add them to the design.

Design tip

To make it last keep the arrangement in the fridge when it is not displayed.

Pomegranate trio

You will need

- **3 pomegranates (*Punica*)**
- **3 red roses (I have used *Rosa* 'Grand Prix')**
- **rose hips**
- **9 stems flexi grass**
- **apple slices (optional)**

Design tip

For a frosted effect you could first dip the pomegranates in a stiff egg white solution and then in caster sugar.

These luscious fruits provide an excellent source of moisture for three perfect roses.

Method

1 Make a hole in the top of each pomegranate with a knife or apple corer.

2 Cut each rose short and place in the hole together with a sprig of hips or berries.

3 Cut the flexi grass and loop this to join two of the pomegranates together. Repeat with other stems to create a triangular composition.

4 As an option scatter dried apple slices at the base of the fruits and place on a platter.

Spring into autumn

You will need

- deep round container – this one is about 10 cm (4 in) tall
- decorative aluminium wire
- 2 stems of *Gloriosa superba* 'Rothschildiana'

Design tips

The gold of the wire picks up the yellow edges of the *Gloriosa* in this design.

Aluminium wire is available in a rainbow of colours so experiment with the flowers you use. When this arrangement is finished re-use the wire in another design.

It is a bonus when mechanics can be attractive as well as functional so experiment with ways of keeping stems in place. This design uses a coil of aluminium wire to support two delicate stems of *Gloriosa*.

Method

1 Aluminium wire is sold in coils, so just fit one coil into the container and pull it up slightly. Bend the uppermost rings into a spring shape so that that it forms a pyramid.

2 Add water and position the flowers through the coils into the water.

Cabbage patch

Ornamental cabbages (*Brassica*) are a novel material to use in a design. They provide a strong, bold form and like the *Agapanthus* are long-lasting.

You will need

- tall cream container – this one is 20 cm (8 in) in height
- 6.5 cm (2$^1/_2$ in) pinholder
- 4-6 *Agapanthus*
- raffia
- 3-4 ornamental cabbages (*Brassica*)

Design tips

Brassica will begin to smell so make sure you change the water regularly to keep it clear of bacteria. Remove any outer leaves as they turn yellow and the cabbages will last for weeks.

If you do not have a pinholder you could use floral foam instead.

Method

1 Place the pinholder in the container. Add water.

2 Arrange the *Agapanthus* in the hand so that their heads form a rounded mass. Cut the stems level. Tie them together using the raffia, about 10-15 cm down the stem and again close to the stem ends.

3 Push the bunch firmly onto the pinholder.

4 Cut the *Brassica* so that their heads rest on the rim of the container and arrange them around the stems of the *Agapanthus*.

Allium lollipop

The giant *Allium*, which is part of the onion family, grows easily in the garden but is also available at the florist during the summer and autumn.

Method

1 If the container is not waterproof then line with a piece of black bin liner.

2 Place the pinholder at the bottom of the container and fill with water. Alternatively, use foam.

3 Cut the stem of the *Allium* so that once positioned in the container the whole will be approximately three times the height of the container.

4 Cut the stems of *Skimmia* short and angle them out of the foam or pinholder. You will need longer stems if using a pinholder.

5 Hold the end of the two wool lengths and wrap these around the *Allium* stem neatly. Tuck the ends in on themselves or tie at the back.

You will need

· container (see design tip below) – this one is 18 cm (7 in) tall
· pinholder or floral foam
· 1 stem *Alllum giganteum*
· *Skimmia* or other foliage with a regular form
· 2 lengths of tapestry wool to pick up the lime of the leaves and the purple of the *Allium*

Design tips

To get good visual balance, your chosen container should have a volume approximately equal to the volume of the *Allium* head.

***Skimmia* is an excellent evergreen shrub to grow in the garden and is easy to root from cuttings. It produces flowers and/or berries, depending on the variety, for many months of the year.**

17

- a flat dish in a dark colour – this one is 30 cm (12 in) in diameter
- 3-5 aubergines
- 5-7 *Cobaea scandens*
- small orchid tubes
- flat plain leaves – I have used *Heuchera* but you could use geranium or blackberry leaves

Design tips

Be aware that if the orchid tubes are resting on their sides then the stems may not be completely submerged in water.

If an orchid tube is visible then spray it with adhesive spray mount and wrap an ivy leaf around.

Cobaea scandens

Also known as the cup and saucer vine, this beautiful climbing plant has deep purple blooms that match the rich tones of the aubergines. Although difficult to propagate from seed *Cobaea scandens* will self-seed year after year once established.

Method

1 Arrange the aubergines in a pile on the plate.

2 Add water to the orchid tubes and place one flower or leaf in each.

3 Bury the tubes amongst the aubergines so that they are hidden from view.

Woven leaves

You will need

- **dark coloured container with a square opening – this one is 10 cm (4 in) wide and 20 cm (8 in) tall**
- **floral foam**
- **1 stem of Kentia palm (*Howea forsteriana*) or *Phoenix* date palm**
- **florists' steel or decorative headed pins**
- **1 bloom of lily (*Lilium*)**

Design tips

You could use any long thin leaf for this design. If you have the patience then try something like lily or China grass.

When taking individual leaves from a larger frond always take from the bottom first. You are left with a tip which is much easier to use elsewhere.

This technique is fiddly, but once mastered looks fabulous and can be recreated on any scale.

Method

1 Fill the container with foam so that it is level with the rim.

2 Pull individual leaves from the palm. Lay them vertically across the container so that the foam is covered.

3 Take another leaf and weave it horizontally through the vertical leaves so that it goes over one leaf and under the next.

4 Repeat this process but with the second leaf start by going under the first vertical leaf and over the second so that it is the opposite of your first horizontal placement. Continue until the foam is covered.

5 Pin the woven leaves to the foam so that it is secure.

6 Push the lily between the woven leaves and into the foam.

Burnished gold

This front-facing design is warm, fiery, and totally autumnal.

You will need

- tall, natural coloured container – this one is 25 cm (10 in) tall
- floral foam
- 5 bloom *Chrysanthemum* in orange or gold
- spray paint in metallic shades (optional)
- 3-5 large *Hydrangea*
- large *Fatsia* leaves
- fire thorn (*Pyracantha*)

Design tips

The thorns of the *Pyracantha* are extremely sharp so wear gloves when handling.

Fatsia is an easy shrub to grow in the garden – it is evergreen and will provide structural leaves for designs all year round.

Method

1 Soak the foam and wedge it into the container, so that it rises about 20 percent above the rim.

2 Cut one *Chrysanthemum* so that when placed in the foam it rises one and a half times the height of the container above its rim. Add the other chrysanthemums to the design at varying heights.

3 Using the spray paints, lightly burnish the *Hydrangea* and *Fatsia* leaves. Make sure you are in a well ventilated area.

4 Add the *Hydrangea* to the design to reinforce the shape you have created with the *Chrysanthemum*. Place the *Fatsia* leaves at the back to frame the design.

5 Place the *Pyracantha* throughout to lift the colours and bring out the metallic shades.

You will need

- cube vase – the one used is 12 cm (5 in) square
- floral foam
- snake grass (*Equisetum hyemale*)
- 4 roses
- twigs or thin stems (dried or fresh)
- 4 carnations (*Dianthus*)

Design tips

Try and keep the width of the design uniform from top to bottom to make it structured and compact.

I like to cut foam when it is wet as fewer dust particles are released but it does sometimes generate more waste.

Snake in the grass

Snake grass (*Equisetum hyemale*) is a wonderful material to work with – it is hollow and easily manipulated. This layered design uses the linear movement created by the snake grass and dogwood (*Cornus*) to give a column effect.

Method

1 Soak your foam. Cut it so that when placed in the container there is a gap on each of the four sides to insert the snake grass. The foam should be level with the rim of the container.

2 Cut the snake grass into lengths just taller than the foam. Insert them between the foam and the container (not into the foam).

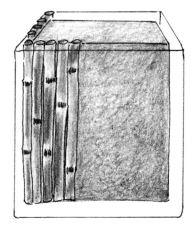

3 Add the four roses at the centre of the design. The distance between the base of the rose and the rim should be approximately the same as the height of the container.

4 Add the twigs or stems in amongst the roses. The height of the twigs above the rim should be approximately twice the height of the container.

5 If your carnations are tight, blow on them gently and tease out the petals to make them bigger.

6 Cut the carnations short and add them at the base of the design to cover the visible foam and add texture.

Blooming blues

Contemporary containers with strong form and colour demand dramatic flowers, foliage and style.

You will need

- contemporary container in a bold colour. I have used a 18 cm (7 in) high half-moon container with a 30 cm (12 in) x 10 cm (4 in) opening
- sticky tape
- 5 blue *Hydrangea*
- lily grass (*Liriope gigantea*)
- variegated *Aspidistra* leaves
- florists' fix

Design tip

If you decide to substitute the *Hydrangea* in this design with another flower then you may have more trouble securing the loops of lily grass. You could try wiring the loop ends together or securing them with fix.

Method

1 Add water to the container, making sure the outside is dry.

2 Using the sticky tape, create a grid over the top of the container (see Techniques page 94).

3 Cut the stems of the *Hydrangea* so that their heads will rest on the rim of the container and add them to the design.

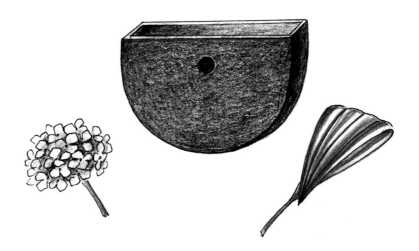

4 Create the loops of lily grass by pushing each end into the container, through the *Hydrangea* heads. As the hydrangeas are a mass of petals, the lily grass should stay in place.

5 Bend the *Aspidistra* leaves in half and secure using a little florists' fix. Add these to the design.

Design tip

Variegated *Aspidistra* are not always available from the florist but any *Aspidistra* leaf will work well. If you cannot find these at your florist buy a pot plant and cut when needed.

Chocolate cosmos

Cosmos atrosanguineus has a mild vanilla fragrance which along with its rich dark colour contributes to its common name – chocolate cosmos.

You will need

- wreath made of plant material such as twigs or straw – this one is 33 cm (13 in) in diameter
- low plate or round tray – this will not be seen so it does not need to be attractive. It should be about the same size as the wreath or slightly smaller.
- thick pillar candle in a dark colour – this one is 10 cm (4 in) tall.
- quinces (*Chaenomeles*) or small apples (*Malus*)
- 10-12 chocolate cosmos (*Cosmos atrosanguineus*)
- cotton wool
- tinfoil or clingfilm

Method

1 Position the wreath on the plate and place the candle in the centre.

2 Fill the space between with the quinces or apples.

3 Soak small pieces of cotton wool in water and wrap around the end of the flower stems. Wrap a piece of tinfoil or clingfilm over the cotton wool to secure and hold in the moisture.

Design tip

Whilst beautiful, *Cosmos* will only live a few days. The rest of this design will last so you can simply replace the flowers when they fade.

4 Carefully insert the stems of *Cosmos* between the apples so that their heads are attractively displayed.

Encircled

You will need

- foam ring – this one is 24 cm (9 in) in diameter
- medium sized pumpkin
- 7-10 stems *Chrysanthemum* in a variety of sizes and autumn colours

Design tips

Make sure you angle the lower flowers downwards to hide the polystyrene base of the foam ring.

You could wrap a length of seasonal ribbon around the base of the ring.

Chrysanthemum come in a myriad of forms, sizes and colours and when combined together give an exciting and bold display.

Method

1 Soak the foam ring by lowering into a deep bowl of water at a slight angle for about 60 seconds.

2 Chamfer the edges of the foam, removing the sharp edges with a knife (see Techniques page 92).

3 Place the pumpkin in the centre of the ring. If you feel it is too low then raise it by placing it on a small upturned dish or saucer.

4 Add the chrysanthemums to cover the ring completely. You should create blocks and patterns of colour, form and texture.

Autumn lanterns

Amaryllis are often associated with Christmas but they come into season in the autumn. *Physalis* dry well and retain their colour so you can use these sunny lanterns all year round.

Method

1 Bind the amaryllis together with a rubber band so that their heads form a round mass. Hide the rubber band by wrapping with decorative wire. Cut the stems level.

2 Place the pinholder centrally in the bottom of the bowl. Impale the stem ends of the amaryllis down onto the pinholder so that they stand vertically.

3 Add the pebbles to the base so that the pinholder is covered.

4 To make the hoops of *Physalis* place a short length of wire in one end, then bend the stem round. Place over the rim of the container and insert the wire into the other end of the stem to secure. The stems should be cut at a wide enough point to allow insertion of the wire.

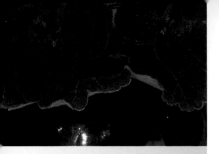

Nasturtium night light

Unassuming garden flowers which would be lost in a large container can be beautiful in small designs. The candle means that this arrangement would be perfect to light up a dinner table.

You will need

· **small round container –
  this one is approximately
  10 cm (4 in) diameter**
· **floral foam**
· **small candle**
· **cocktail sticks**
· **florists' tape**
· **decorative wire**
· **6-8 *Nasturtium* with their
  leaves**

Design tips

**Make several of these
and place down the
centre of a dinner table.
Make sure that the
candle is high enough so
that when lit it the
flowers will not burn.**

**Nasturtiums are one of
the easiest flowers to
grow and the poorer the
soil the more prolific the
flowering.**

Method

1 Add water to the container. Cut a piece of soaked foam that will fit inside to just above the rim. This is to support the candle.

2 Wrap the base of the candle with the decorative wire.

3 Add the flowers and leaves around the candle making sure their stems are in the foam. Keep the arrangement topped up with water.

Pumpkin parade

These designs would be ideal for a Halloween party lined up along the table. They are simple to create and will last for weeks.

Method

1 Line the containers with plastic bin liner and trim so that there is no excess above the rim.

2 Wedge the soaked foam into the containers so that it rises slightly above the rim.

3 Place one mini gourd on the top of the foam in each container.

4 Add sprigs of beech around the base of the gourd, angled downwards over the rim of the container.

5 Finish with a row of chrysanthemums between the base of the gourd and the leaves.

You will need

· terracotta 'long tom' containers – these are 12 cm (5 in) tall
· plastic bin liner for lining the containers
· floral foam
· mini gourds with flat bases
· fresh or preserved beech (*Fagus*)
· 2 stems 'Santini' *Chrysanthemum*

Design tips

Chrysanthemums are available in a range of lovely autumnal colours so you can mix and match.

If you wish to preserve beech, the process is quick, easy and effective (see Techniques page 97).

Pins and needles

Contemporary and stylish, this design uses minimal plant material for maximum impact.

You will need

- orange Perspex® or glass cube container – the one used is 15 cm (6 in) square
- 4 pincushion protea (*Leucospermum*)
- coloured aluminium wire
- florists' fix

Design tips

The idea of using coiled aluminium wire around the base would also work with roses, hydrangeas or any other flower with a strong, robust stem.

Make sure that the container is completely dry and clean when you add the flowers so that the fix will stick properly.

Method

1 Cut the pincushion protea short. Wrap the bottom of each stem with aluminium wire, making a wider spiral at the base.

2 Push a ball of fix onto the base of each flower so that it is predominately hidden by the aluminium wire. This may not be necessary if the flowers are well balanced on their stem.

3 Place the flowers into the container so that they stand upright.

4 Add a small amount of water.

Ring of roses

As the nights draw in the glow of a candle brings welcome light and warmth to a room.

You will need

- **round basket container lined with plastic bin liner to make it waterproof – this one is 20 cm (8 in) in diameter**
- **floral foam**
- **sharp knife**
- **spoon**
- **thick candle – this should fill about half of the container**
- **glass with the same circumference as the candle**
- **10-12 small roses – these are *Rosa* 'Leonidas'**
- **1 stem brown *Hypericum***
- **florists' fix**

Take care

Remember to remove the berries as the candle burns down.

Never leave a lighted candle unattended.

Method

1 Shape the foam using a sharp knife so that it fits snugly inside the container but allowing a small space for the addition of water.

2 Place the glass upside-down on the foam and press down on it so that it cuts through the foam to create an indented circle. With the spoon, remove foam to the depth required so that the candle will be at a suitable height.

3 Put the foam in the container and push the candle into the hole in the centre so that it is secure.

4 Cut the roses short and place them in the foam around the base of the candle so that only the heads show.

5 Add sprigs of *Hypericum* between the roses to hide the foam.

6 Place a miniscule piece of fix behind a *Hypericum* berry with the stalk removed. Adhere the back of the berry to the candle and repeat around the candle at regular intervals.

Roll up

You will need

- low rectangular dish – this one is 30 cm (12 in) long
- strips of rolled bark
- orchid tubes
- 8-10 calla lilies (*Zantedeschia*)

Design tips

You could insert any flower in the rolls but those with a strong sculptural form and smooth stems will work best. Consider *Anthurium*, mini *Gerbera*, dahlias and even nasturtiums. Their colours will harmonise well with the bark.

Plane trees are to be found in many city streets as they absorb pollution happily, and their bark is an interesting and beautiful feature.

Trees such as the birch have beautiful bark which can sometimes be found in strips on the forest floor by fallen trees. Bark such as *Eucalyptus* can also be purchased from a specialist shop.

The plane tree regularly discards its bark in rolled sections and is therefore ideal for this design.

Method

1 Arrange the bark on the plate in parallel lines.

2 Fill orchid tubes two thirds full with water and insert one calla into each.

3 Slightly loosen the rolls of bark and place the tubes within so that the flower heads protrude.

Ball of blooms

Almost all flowers look impressive when massed together, even the inexpensive long lasting *Chrysanthemum*. Surrounded by artichokes the flower ball is a shot of glorious colour.

You will need

- low bowl or dish – this one is 30 cm (12 in) wide
- sphere of foam – this one was 9 cm (3½ in) in diameter
- 8-10 stems of spray *Chrysanthemum*
- 8-10 artichokes

Design tips

If you wish the sphere to appear bigger, place an inverted small dish or saucer in the bottom of the dish and place the sphere on top.

Try this design with carnations or spray carnations.

Method

1. Soak the foam sphere. Remove as soon as it has sunk to become level with the water.

2. Cut a thin slice off one side of the foam to form the base. Cover the sphere in chrysanthemums. Leave the area at the base of the sphere empty.

3. Arrange the artichokes around the ball of chrysanthemums in the dish, so that their stems are hidden beneath.

Aubergine dream

These wonderful pink and cream variegated aubergines were found in a French supermarket. Searching out unusual vegetables, particularly in the autumn, is a great hobby.

You will need

· round plate – this one is 30 cm (12 in) in diameter
· 5-7 aubergines
· 1 stem of *Phalaenopsis* with approximately 5 flower heads
· orchid tubes

Design tip

Making the aubergines stay where you want them is quite a balancing act. If they really will not behave then use florists' fix or double-sided tape to secure them. Alternatively, place a tall thin piece of floral foam centrally on the plate and lean the aubergines onto this support. You could skewer them with kebab sticks for additional support.

Method

1 Arrange the aubergines on the plate so that their heads are resting together in a tepee shape.

2 Remove one of the lower heads of the *Phalaenopsis* and put it aside. Pour some water in the orchid tube and insert the stem of *Phalaenopsis.* Carefully insert the tube into the gap at the top of the aubergines.

3 Place the shorter stem into another orchid tube and rest it at the bottom of the design so that the tube is hidden. This takes the eye through to the base of the design.

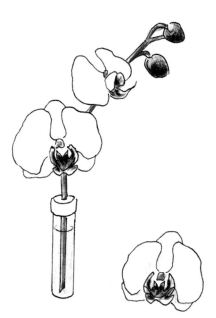

Black and white

You will need

· **tall black or dark brown container** – this one is 25 cm (10 in) tall
· **floral foam**
· **5-7 white pompom** *Dahlia*
· *Heuchera* **leaves**

Design tips

Be careful with visual balance. The arrangement must not look like it might topple over. Here the use of a larger flower at the base of the arrangement stops it from looking top heavy.

If you do not have *Heuchera* **leaves use Boston ivy (***Parthenocissus tricuspidata***) or ivy leaves.**

Do not be afraid of creating contrast in your designs. Black and white look great together and give a stunning effect.

Method

1 Wedge the soaked floral foam into the container so that it is level with the rim.

2 Place the *Dahlia* in the foam at varying heights. The tallest stem should be about one and a half times the height of the container.

3 Cover the foam and frame the stems using the *Heuchera* leaves.

Sphere of influence

Lichen covered foam provides an exciting container for the flowers of your choice.

Method

1 Arrange the pebbles on the plate.

2 If you do not have a foam sphere, cut a square of foam and make a roughly spherical shape with your hands. Wash your hands afterwards to remove all the dust particles. Cut off a sliver of foam to create a flat base.

3 Soak the foam sphere and then cover it in lichen, securing with the pins.

4 Arrange on the plate with the pebbles and insert the stems of *Gloriosa* into the top of the sphere.

You will need

· **dark coloured plate – this one is 30 cm (12 in) in diameter**
· **pebbles**
· **foam sphere or piece of foam carved into a ball**
· **dried lichen**
· **mossing pins or wire bent into hairpins (see Techniques page 96)**
· **2 stems of *Gloriosa***

Design tips

You could use mini *Gerbera*, *Chrysanthemum* 'Shamrock' or dahlias in place of the *Gloriosa*.

Be sure that the flowers you use are not so heavy that they tip the sphere. Use the pebbles to keep it in place or place fix on the bottom of a frog and insert in the base of the sphere (see Techniques page 92).

47

A posy of roses

You will need

- **round container – this one is 15 cm (6 in) tall.**
- **10-12 red roses or mini *Gerbera***
- **garden twine**
- **5-7 large ivy or small *Fatsia* leaves**

Design tips

Garden twine has a rough surface and is easier to use than smooth textured string.

When creating your bouquet stand facing square to your work surface. If you hold your flowers to one side your bouquet has more chance of being lop-sided.

As a table centrepiece or a heartfelt gift this arrangement of massed red roses is sure to give pleasure.

Method

1 Arrange the roses or mini *Gerbera* one at a time in your hand with their stems parallel, until you have created a slightly rounded mass that is equal on all sides. Keep turning the bunch in your hands to get good balance.

2 Tie the roses securely with twine.

3 Add the ivy or *Fatsia* leaves around the edge of the roses to form a frill, then tie again.

4 Cut all the stems level.

5 Half fill your container with water and add your flowers.

Orange glow

The wonderful versatile *Hydrangea* surrounds as group of vibrant 'Cherry Brandy' roses in this structured design.

You will need

- tall vase – this one is 17.5 cm (7 in) tall
- 5-7 *Rosa* 'Cherry Brandy'
- 5-7 garden hydrangeas
- about 7 *Aspidistra* leaves
- about 10 stems flexi grass

Design tip

Rosa 'Cherry Brandy' is a particularly gorgeous orange rose with a touch of pink/orange on the outer petals. You could also use *Rosa* 'Milva' or *Rosa* 'Naranga' or change the mood completely by adding a deep pink or bright red rose.

Method

1 Remove the foliage and thorns carefully from the roses leaving the top set of leaves on the stem.

2 Group the roses in the hand keeping the stems straight.

3 Clean the stems of the hydrangeas and place in a circle around the roses.

4 Use the flexi grass in twos. Thread one end down between the roses and the hydrangeas. Loop the grass and bring the ends over the hydrangea heads and down. Grip tightly and when all the ends are in place bind with twine just under the heads.

5 Place the tied bunch in your vase.

6 Manipulate the *Aspidistra* leaves (see Techniques page 97) and tuck around the hydrangeas so that they frame the flowers.

Pumpkin panache

You will need

- a square container – this one is 18 cm (7 in) square
- a piece of floral foam
- a small pumpkin that will not overwhelm the container
- a selection of flowers with a round form such as carnations, open roses, dahlias, mini gerbera
- green foliage to unify the flowers – here I have used *Skimmia* but you could use bay, ivy or box

Design tips

Penetrating the skin of the pumpkin will shorten its life.

In the spring you could replace the pumpkin with a chocolate egg, and at Christmas with a large glass bauble.

This design using a few flowers from the florist, foliage from the garden and topped with a pumpkin from the supermarket or allotment would be suitable for Halloween or harvest.

Method

1   Cut the foam so that it rises above the rim of the container. Soak the foam. Leave space so that water can easily be added.

2   Place the pumpkin in the centre of the foam. If you have chosen a pumpkin with a flat bottom it will rest there quite securely. You could place lengths of kebab stick through the pumpkin and into the foam.

3   Create one group of flowers for example roses. Build up the design by punctuating the space around the pumpkin with groups of flowers. Fill in the spaces between with your foliage.

You will need

- black cube container – this one is 12 cm (5 in) square
- sycamore wings
- florists' fix
- 7-10 yellow bloom chrysanthemums

Design tip

I have used yellow chrysanthemums to pick up the colour in the sycamore wings. If you are lucky you can find the wings in some beautiful reds and pinks, and you could change the colour of the *Chrysanthemum* accordingly.

Sunshine

Bloom chrysanthemums are at their best in the autumn and this yellow variety will brighten up any room. The vase is adorned with some detached sycamore wings that are found on the ground beneath sycamore trees in the early autumn.

Method

1   Take two detached sycamore wings and stick them together using a tiny amount of florists' fix.

2   Adhere the jointed wings to the container and repeat to make a pattern of your choice. You should not need to add any more fix.

3   Fill the container with water and add your chrysanthemums. Arrange them so that they form a dome shape.

Gaudy gourds

Almost too bright to look at, this plate of gourds is given a touch of class with the addition of a single dahlia.

Method

1 Arrange the gourds on the plate so that they look attractive.

2 Place individual *Physalis* heads in amongst the gourds.

3 Fill the orchid tube with water and push the stem of the *Dahlia* inside. Add to your plate of gourds.

Arti-choked

You will need

- **two similar containers in a dark colour, with letterbox shaped openings – these are 20 cm (8 in) and 30 cm (10 in) tall**
- **floral foam**
- **artichokes – enough to fill the top of the containers**
- **crab-apples (*Malus*)**
- **medium gauge florists' wire**

Design tip

You could also use cherries or cherry tomatoes on and off the vine in this design, although you may have to improvise!

This fun design does not actually contain any flowers. It will however, provide a talking point at any dinner party.

Method

1 Wedge floral foam into the opening of both containers making sure it is not visible above the rim.

2 Push the stems of the artichokes into the foam so that they are all at the same height.

3 Place one crab-apple on top of each artichoke by pushing its stalk in between the leaves.

4 Bend a piece of wire into a narrow 'S' shape. Hook one end over the rim of the container and hang a bunch of crab-apples over the other.

Apple jack

This innovative design uses apples instead of foam to give the roses moisture and to keep them in position.

Method

1 Place a few leaves in each cube.

2 Cut the stems of the roses to a sharp point and push one Into the top of each apple.

3 Place the apples into the vases.

You will need

· **3 small cube vases –
  these are 10 cm (4 in)
  square**
· **3 apples**
· **3 roses in a colour to
  match the apples**
· **dried leaves such as
  oak or horse chestnut**

Design tip

**There is enough moisture
in the apple to sustain
the rose for several days.
You may wish to take the
roses out and give them
a drink occasionally to
make them last. If they
wilt then use the revival
technique mentioned in
'Caring for your flowers'
on page 100.**

Thanksgiving wreath

A festive wreath for the front door that is full of warmth and movement.

You will need

- a plain twiggy wreath – this one is 30 cm (12 in) in diameter
- 7 *Rosa* 'Grand Prix'
- 7 small orchid tubes
- thick aluminium wire
- about 20 apple slices
- 2-3 mini pumpkins
- about 20 stems corn
- 1 stem Chinese lanterns (*Physalis*)
- 1 stem of beech (preserved or fresh)
- a few autumnal leaves
- medium gauge florists' wires

Design tips

Be careful adding the mini pumpkins as they are visually heavy and need to be balanced by other material.

Keep the orchid tubes topped up with water.

If you want to hang the wreath use strong twine or raffia covered wire.

Method

1 Prepare the components for your wreath.

   a) Leaving a straight length of approximately 8 cm (3 in) free, start at the top and wrap thick aluminium wire around each orchid tube. The free length will be used to penetrate the wreath and keep the tube in place. Fill the tube two thirds with water and insert a cut rose in each.

   b) Group a few apple slices together and wire with a stalk long enough to be pushed through the wreath.

   c) Insert 2 or 3 lengths of wire into the base of the mini pumpkins.

   d) Cut the stems of corn short. Wrap the wire carefully around a group of three or four stems and leave a wire stalk long enough to be pushed through the wreath.

   e) Cut the Chinese lanterns into short lengths, each with its own stalk.

2 Place all the components in the wreath by pushing the wires deep into the wreath. If they are long enough to come out the far side bend the wires back into the wreath.

3 Fill in any gaps with autumn leaves.

Very berry

You will need

- letterbox shaped container – this one is black glass and approximately 30 cm (12 in) long
- berries on stems such as *Viburnum opulus* 'Roseum' and privet (*Ligustrum*)
- 1 red *Dahlia*

Design tip

You could of course use foam for this design, but be careful not to make it look too regimented. It should have a loose natural appearance.

You could defoliate the berried branches for a more dramatic, contemporary design.

The hedgerows are full of berries in autumn and there is nothing like them for providing gloss and texture.

Method

1 Add some water to the container.

2 Place the berry stems in the container one at a time so that they form a balanced mass. As you add more stems they will begin to overlap in the vase and support one another.

3 Add the *Dahlia* to the centre of the arrangement.

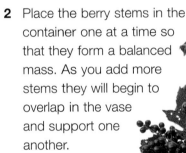

A touch of exotica

This design mixes traditional plant material with a touch of exotica from South Africa.

You will need

- round deep container – this one is 7.5 cm (3 in) deep and 28 cm (11 in) in diameter
- plastic bin liner to line the container if there is a possibility of leakage
- soaked floral foam
- beech leaves
- about 20 fir cones
- 8-10 pincushion proteas (*Leucospermum*)
- 4-6 carnations
- 1 stem Singapore orchids
- decorative beads (optional)
- thin decorative aluminium wire

Design tips

Spray the orchids with water to keep them fresh.

I have used stabilized/ preserved beech from the florist. You can create your own easily. See Techniques on page 97.

Method

1 Cut the bin liner to fill the inside of the container.

2 Soak the foam and place in the container so that it is level with the rim and with space for the easy addition of water.

3 Place short sprigs of beech around the circumference of the container.

4 Wire the fir cones and repeat the circular positioning of the beech.

5 Repeat with the pincushion protea and finish with the carnations. Try and achieve a slightly domed effect.

6 Remove the individual flowers from the stem of Singapore orchids. Thread the heads onto the length of wire taking the end through the base of the flowers. Intersperse with a few beads if you so wish. Drape over the arrangement.

Daring dahlias

Dahlias come in some fantastic colours. They are not around for very long so make the most of them by massing them together for a blast of rich, hot colour.

You will need

- glass vase approximately 20 cm (8 in) tall
- glass dish – this one is 25 cm (10 in) in diameter. It has concave sides but this is not essential.
- dahlias in a variety of hot colours
- bunch of steel grass (*Xanphorrhoea*) or bear grass (*Xerophyllum*)
- 16-20 mini peppers in a variety of colours – red, orange and yellow

Design tips

These peppers will last longer if you keep them in the fridge when you are not using them.

If you cannot find mini peppers you could use anything that reflects the hot colour of the dahlias such as tomatoes, chilli peppers or star fruit.

Method

1 Place the vase inside the dish. If it wobbles then secure it with a little fix. Add some water to the vase.

2 Wind the bunch of steel grass around the inside of the dish and place the peppers on top.

3 Arrange the dahlias in the glass vase so that they form an even mass.

Caged in

Equisitum hyemale (snakegrass) provides the ideal fence for a host of golden chrysanthemums.

You will need

- round low glass bowl – this one is 7.5 cm (3 in) tall and 18 cm (7 in) in diameter
- floral foam
- 1 bunch *Equisitum hyemale*
- 5 stems spray chrysanthemums
- 3 stems *Hypericum*

Design tips

Instead of the *Equisitum* use dogwood (*Cornus*), bamboo or any straight stems cut into uniform lengths.

You could substitute roses, gerberas or any round flower for the chrysanthemums.

Method

1 Prepare the foam so that it rises a couple of centimetres (1 in) above the rim of the container. It should fit into the container so that there is sufficient space around to fit in the *Equisitum*. If too much space is left the stems will be difficult to keep in position upright.

2 Cut the *Equisitum* stems into uniform lengths so that they are slightly taller than the foam and tuck between the glass and the foam.

3 Take the flowers from the main stem of the chrysanthemum, on their secondary stems, and create a gently domed mass of flowers. Angle the bottom flowers over the tops of the *Equisitum.*

4 Thread the individual *Hypericum* berries onto wire and balance on the rim of the glass container. Twist the wire ends together and tuck into a stem of *Equisitum* to hide.

Corn wrap

Dried corn provides the perfect container for a Thanksgiving arrangement.

You will need

· **straight sided container – this one is 18 cm (7 in) tall and 20 cm (8 in) in diameter**
· **about 15 dried corns**
· **extra strong thick rubber bands**
· **raffia**
· **plastic bin liner**
· **soaked floral foam**
· **5-7 sunflowers**
· **gourds**
· **hips or berries**
· ***Sedum***
· **roses, gerberas or more of any of the above ingredients to fill your design**

Design tip

Sedum is a wonderful autumn flower which dries on the stem. The red-brown dried flowers provide a rough texture and good autumn colouring which will last once cut.

Method

1 Place the rubber bands over the top of the container.

2 If the husks of the corn are long cut these with scissors to give a uniform appearance. Tuck the corn around the container under the rubber bands. Manipulate the rubber bands so that one is closer to the top of the corn and the other closer to the bottom.

3 Cover the rubber bands with raffia. This will also give extra security to the corn.

4 Line the container with bin liner if there is any chance of leakage.

5 Place the soaked foam in the container so that it is level with the rim of the container.

6 Starting with the sunflowers, group your flowers and berries so that they radiate from the centre of the foam. Your aim is to create a gently rounded mass of plant material with little or no space between the elements.

7 Position the gourds on the design to give a contrast of form and texture. Wiring most gourds is nigh impossible so just balance them by placing them at a judicious angle.

Off-kilter

Your designs do not always have to be symmetrically balanced. Asymmetric balance is harder to achieve successfully but can look totally sophisticated.

You will need

· **lime green container – this one is 20 cm (8 in) tall**
· **3-5 red roses such as** *Rosa* **'Grand Prix'**
· **string or garden twine**
· **1 large exotic leaf. I have used** *Anthurium crystellinum*

Design tip

Alternative leaves could be *Monstera, Fatsia, Strelitzia* **– all long lasting evergreen leaves.**

Method

1 Add water to the container.
2 Arrange the roses in your hand so that their heads are massed together. Tie them together just under their heads with the string or garden twine.
3 Cut the stems of the bunch you have created so that when placed in the container, it rests securely on one side.
4 Add the leaf to the other side of the container, tucking the part where the leaf meets the stem around the roses.

Fine wine

These simple wreath arrangements of everlasting flowers will dry in situ and last for months. Once the wine has been enjoyed, place a candle in the neck and continue the display.

You will need

- foam ring – these are 20 cm (8 in) in diameter
- a bunch of winged statice (*Limonium sinuatum*) for each ring

Design tips

You can use dry or fresh *Limonium* in this design. Use the foam dry or soaked accordingly. Dried statice is easier to insert in the foam than fresh.

Avoid trying to place large sprays in the design. Keep the sprigs short and neat to give a rounded even shape to the ring.

You could use small poppy seedheads or sprigs of mature *Hydrangea* to create attractive alternative wreaths.

Method

1 Chamfer the edges of the ring so that you will achieve a more rounded shape.

2 Cut the *Limonium* into tiny sprigs and cover the foam evenly. Try to create a smooth shape by keeping each sprig the same length.

3 Place a wine bottle in the centre of each ring.

Runners and riders

The green of these runner beans is beautiful when combined with the pinky-purple of the *Dahlia*. Green is a neutral colour in flower arranging and will work well with any colour you choose.

You will need

- round container with straight sides – this one is 20 cm (8 in) tall
- 2 *Cordyline* leaves
- runner beans
- 3 *Dahlia*
- orchid tubes

Design tips

The *Cordyline* have a wonderful pink variegation but plain ones will also work well.

The beans I used were those that over-grew whilst I was on holiday – it was either working them into a design or putting them straight into the compost!

Method

1 Place the *Cordyline* leaves inside the container so that they are flat against the sides. You may have to remove the stalks in order to do this.

2 Fill the container with the runner beans. Do not try to be too neat about this – they should look like a chaotic mass.

3 Put some water in each orchid tube and put one *Dahlia* in each. Bury these amongst the beans so that the flowers are shown to their best advantage.

Full of beans

Materials such as the kidney beans used in this design provide colour and texture at little expense. They can be used again and again and are useful for hiding foam and other mechanics.

You will need

· glass container – the one used has a flower pot shape and is 15 cm (6 in) tall
· kidney beans
· plastic dish to fit the top of the container
· floral foam
· florists' tape
· *Eucalyptus cineraria*
· 5-6 roses – I have used *Rosa 'Aqua'*
· *Scabiosa*
· *Heuchera* leaves
· snowberry (*Symphoricarpos*)
· mixed foliage (optional)

Design tip

You could put the foam directly into the container and pour the kidney beans around it. However, if the kidney beans get wet they will rapidly become mouldy and not last long.

Method

1 Fill the glass container with kidney beans.

2 Place the plastic dish in the top of the glass container. Secure a block of soaked foam into the dish using florists' tape.

3 Create an outline with the *Eucalyptus* and other foliage (see Techniques page 93). Add the roses, *Scabiosa* and snowberry evenly throughout the design.

Conkers

You will need

· a plate or dish – this one is 18 cm (7 in) in diameter and copper but you could use any rich colour
· one or several thick white candles
· horse chestnuts (aka 'conkers' from the *Aesculus hippocastanum* tree) some in their shells, some out

Design tips

Depending on how many conkers you find, you can scale this design up or down. It would look spectacular on a huge serving dish or tray with hundreds of piled up horse chestnuts.

You can varnish conkers so that they keep longer.

If you wanted you could add fir cones, nuts and/or Chinese lanterns to the display – they will all last in good condition for the whole season.

Conkers are everywhere in September and October. There is nothing more satisfying than spying an un-opened shell which can be cracked open to reveal the smooth, mahogany coloured horse chestnut.

Method

1 Place the candle(s) in the centre of the plate.

2 Arrange the conkers around the base of the candles.

3 Never leave lighted candles unattended.

Autumn warmth

You will need

- **low dish or plate with high sides – this is 30 cm (12 in) in diameter**
- **square piece of floral foam 15 cm (6 in) square if dish is as above**
- **about 50 larch cones**
- **light to medium gauge florists' wires**
- **10 bloom chrysanthemums**
- **length of decorative wire**
- **couple of autumn leaves**

Design tips

If you first cover your wet foam with plastic bin liner there will be no need to place the arrangement on a dish or platter.

You can use pine cones instead of larch cones but as these are larger the wire you use must be stronger. The weight of the pine cones makes the container a little harder to create.

You can create a novel container with larch cones to hold your favourite autumnal flowers.

Method

1 Cut the four edges off the square piece of foam to form a rough disk. Rub the foam with your hands to create a smoother shape. Soak the foam.

2 Wire each cone by wrapping a wire around the lowest scales of the cone (see Techniques page 95).

3 Starting at the bottom insert the wire stalks into the foam. Work up the foam offsetting the next layer to the one before.

4 Cut the blooms short and insert into the foam so that the heads come down over the rim of the cone container. Create a gently rounded form.

5 Roll small leaves or sections of larger leaves in the hands. Thread on to the decorative wire. Repeat at intervals along the wire. Drape over the flowers.

Ring of roses

Six roses, candles and a few leaves are all that you need to create this contemporary design for the autumn dinner table.

You will need

- **wet foam circle with styrafoam base – this one is 25 cm (10 in) in diameter**
- **4-6 *Aspidistra* leaves (number depending on size)**
- **pins**
- **China grass (*Liriope muscari*)**
- **fine aluminium wire**
- **four red taper candles**
- **cocktail sticks and tape**
- **6 red roses**
- **2 twiggy balls**
- **bun moss**

Design tips

For the ring you need to use the one with a styrafoam base as this is flush with the foam.

Most *Aspidistra* leaves have a more rounded side and a straighter side. Use the straighter side flush with the base and cut any excess from the rounder edge if it is going to swamp your design.

Method

1 Soak the foam circle by immersing in deep water at a slight angle for about 60 seconds.

2 Cut the stems of the *Aspidistra* leaves to about 6 cm (2^1/$_2$ in). Insert one stem end into the foam so the entire stem end is in the foam. Pleat the leaf towards the tip and secure with a pin against the foam.

3 Push a second *Aspidistra* stem into the foam through the folded tip section and again wrap round the foam circle and secure with a pin. Repeat until the outside is covered with leaves. You can also cover the inside of the ring in the same way.

4 Use the China grass decoratively over the *Aspidistra* leaves. Manipulate into bows by looping the grass. Secure in place with a short length of fine wire leaving a wire 'stalk' that can be inserted through the *Aspidistra* leaves into the foam.

5 Create space around the design by looping China grass. If the ends are soft then remove them with scissors – they will then stay in the foam easily.

6 Cover the foam with bun moss.

7 Wrap cocktails sticks around the base of each candle with florists' tape. Insert the candles into the foam in two placements of two, pushing the moss aside if necessary.

8 Cut the roses short and insert in the foam in three groups of two.

9 Add your two twiggy balls.

You will need

- tall container – this one is 25 cm (10 in) high
- foam or a large pinholder
- 12 medium/large sunflowers
- half bunch long steel grass (*Xanthorrhea*)
- rubber bands, florists' tape or twine
- 1-2 stems *Hypericum*
- skeletonized leaves (optional)
- 5-9 *Aspidistra* leaves depending on size

Design tips

You could use beads instead of the *Hypericum* berries.

When the sunflower petals fade they can be removed to give a new look. They are not as cheerful but still look rather interesting.

Sunburst

An explosion of late sunflowers – just right for the festivities on bonfire night.

Method

1 Place the pinholder or soaked foam in the container. If using foam it should rise about half way up the container.

2 Strip the sunflowers of most of their leaves.

3 Hold the steel grass in the hand and group 6 of the sunflowers around the steel grass so that the heads are at the same height. Slip a rubber band up the stems to just below the heads or tie with tape or twine.

4 Take the remaining sunflowers and group at a lower level so that the heads are all the same level. Cut all the stems to the same length leaving sufficient to impale on the pinholder so that the flowers rise well above the rim. If the stems are now short use foam to raise the stems higher.

5 Manipulate the *Aspidistra* leaves (see Techniques page 97). Insert the stem ends in the pinholder or foam.

6 Remove the *Hypericum* berries from the stem and thread onto the end of some of the steel grass. The *Hypericum* will grip the steel grass and stay in place. Thread other steel grass ends onto a few more skeletonized leaves.

Handbags

You will need

- half block of foam
- piece of cellophane or bin liner
- several strands of flexi grass
- medium gauge florists' wire
- decorative wire
- long lasting evenly shaped leaves such as *Eucalyptus cineraria* or hard ruscus (*Danae racemosa*)
- florists' pins
- water spray can
- flowers of choice

Design tip

You can make the bags larger and thinner by using an entire block of foam. Although these would still be suitable as a table decoration check that these are not too heavy for a bride or bridesmaid to carry.

On the catwalk, at the table, or as a bridesmaid's posy this handbag can be used all year round.

Method

1 With a sharp knife cut the foam into a handbag shape. Keep the base about 7.5 cm (3 in) wide at the bottom, 2.5 cm (1 in) at the top and about 10 cm (4 in) tall.

2 Take 2 or 3 strands of flexi grass. Wire each end with a long single legged mount (see Techniques page 96). Push both ends through the top of the foam so it protrudes out of the bottom. Turn the excess wire back into the foam.

3 Embellish the flexi grass with decorative wire if so desired.

4 Spray the foam lightly with water.

5 Cut a piece of cellophane or bin liner to cover the base and to come approximately one third of the way up the sides. Pin in place.

6 Cover the top of the foam with over-lapping leaves. Now work down the bag from the top. The tip of the leaves should stand slightly higher than the top of the foam. Keep a neat regular pattern with the pins. At the bottom tuck any excess leaf under the bag and pin in place.

7 Spray the bag with water.

8 Place a few well conditioned flowers of your choice through the leaves into the foam. You can make a slit in the leaves to make insertion easier.

Techniques

Conditioning plant material

- The ends of all stems that have been out of water, however briefly, seal up. In order to allow a supply of water to enter the stem it must be cut cleanly, at a sharp angle. Use clean, sharp scissors, secateurs or a knife. Take off 2.5 – 5 cm (1-2 in), according to the length of stem. Any foliage that would lie below the water-line or that might enter the foam should also be removed. The stems should be placed immediately in clean containers with fresh, tepid water.

- Add cut flower food to the water, following the instructions on the sachet. Cut flower food allows the flowers to mature fully and last longer. Keep the vase or foam constantly topped up with water. Spraying also helps to keep the plant material fresh. Never hammer the stems, as this encourages rapid bacterial growth.

- Mature foliage can be left under water for an hour or so. Immature and grey foliage quickly becomes waterlogged and should not be immersed. If the foliage is dirty, add a drop of liquid soap but rinse well.

- To revive roses that are wilted rather than old, fill a basin with water, cut the bottom 5 cm (2 in) off the stem and submerge the flower lengthways for 30 minutes.

Colour

Although many books have been written about colour the following are some simple guidelines to help you choose your flowers successfully.

- plain green (i.e. without variegation) is the flower designer's neutral colour and used abundantly will allow nearly all colours to be used together successfully.
- white is a difficult colour to use, whether a white container or a white flower. Use with pastels or deep tones such as burgundy *Leucadendron,* dark brown *Hypericum* berries or blue lisianthus *(Eustoma)* to give depth and interest. Avoid using bright colours (such as pillar box red) which gives too strong a contrast.
- lime green gives zest and vitality to all designs without overpowering or creating discord.
- blue works with all colours but avoid using dark blue and purple in dim lighting. It is a recessive colour and will appear simply as a black hole in dim light or in a large venue. Use yellow and oranges to make a statement in a large or dimly lit setting.

Floral foam

A water absorbing material which supports stems at virtually any angle, floral foam is readily available at DIY stores, florists and larger supermarkets. OASIS® is a well-known brand name. Floral foam is most commonly available as a brick-sized block but is also available in cones, cylinders, rings, spheres and other shapes. There is also a coloured foam called OASIS® Rainbow® Foam. This takes much longer to soak and you will need to add cut flower food.

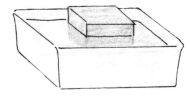

Soaking foam

Measure the size of the piece of foam required and cut it carefully. Place the foam horizontally on water that is deeper than the piece of foam you wish to soak. Allow the foam to sink under its own weight until the top is level with the water and the colour has changed from light to dark green. A block takes approximately 50 seconds to be ready for use. Always keep a reservoir of water in the bottom of your container from which the foam can draw.

Securing foam in a container

To secure foam in a container you can:

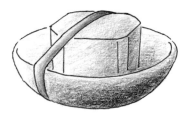

- place florists' fix on the base of a four pronged disc called a 'frog'. Position this on the clean, dry surface of your container and impale your soaked foam on the frog.

and/or

- use florists' tape across the top of your foam and down the two sides of the container.

Chamfering foam

This means removing all the sharp edges to achieve a smoother and more rounded overall shape. It can also allow room for adding water to a finished design.

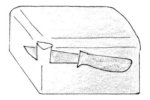

Making a foliage outline

The design on page 78 is based on a strong foundation of foliage. In order to do this effectively it is recommended that:

- the foam rises higher than the container so that stems can be easily angled down over the rim of the container. Then the container and arrangement appear as one, rather than as two separate parts.
- the foliage should appear to radiate from the centre of the foam. In a design where the overall appearance is round, the foliage will radiate like the spokes of a wheel if seen from above.
- a strong three-dimensional form is created by radiating stems from the top of the foam as well as the sides. Again it should appear to originate from the heart of the foam.

Alternative stem supports

Pinholders

Pinholders, or kenzans as they are known in Japan, are stem supports. They are ideal for:

- soft stems that have a need for copious amounts of water such as anemones, turban flowers (*Ranunculus*) and daffodils (*Narcissus*)
- woody stems that are often too heavy to stay happily in place in floral foam, such as lilac (*Syringa*) and guelder rose (*Viburnum opulus* 'Roseum')

Pinholders may be purchased in a wide variety of sizes from the minute 1 cm ($^1/_2$ in) to the large 15 cm (6 in). The most easily found is 6.5 cm ($2^1/_2$ in). A pinholder consists of a multitude of short metal pins in a heavy base which is usually, but not always, round.

Flowers with soft stems can be simply cut and impaled on the pinholder. Woody stems need to be cut at an angle and, if you wish, have a short slit up from the base. The angled cut of the stem should face away from the direction in which the branch is to lean.

Adhesive tape

Transparent adhesive tape can be used to create a grid over the opening of glass containers to give support. You can use tape available from stationers. It will work well as long as it is suitably narrow and the vase is dry. There is also a specialist clear tape available that will adhere to wet surfaces and may be worth buying if you often work with glass.

Tubes

Glass test tubes are a useful way to use flowers in more structural and unusual designs and still provide the water they need. You can also obtain plastic tubes with lids through which a stem can be inserted. These are often used for orchids. These are less attractive but there are various methods of disguising them (such as wrapping them with small leaves or moss). They are available in a variety of sizes. The plastic top means they can be secured at any angle and will not spill their contents. Some glass tubes are now manufactured with holes at the rim for hanging.

Securing candles

Church candles

Place four or five cocktail sticks (cut shorter if the foam is shallow) on a length of florists' tape. The tips should rise just above the tape to give security but not so that it is obvious. Wrap the tape around the candle so that the edge of the tape is on a level with the base of the candle. As an alternative to sticks you could use lengths of thick florists' wire bent into hair pins. The result will be the same.

Standard tapered candles

Use specially manufactured candle holders, which are widely available. If your candle is a little wide, then shave off a small amount with a warm knife. If you do not have a candle holder use the method described above for church candles.

Round or unusually shaped candles

Heat the ends of three heavy-gauge florists' wires, cut down to a suitable length, and ease them into the base of the candle. The heat will soften the wax and allow easy insertion.

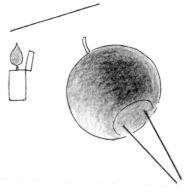

Wiring

Wiring a small cone

a) Take a medium-gauge wire and thread the centre of the wire round the scales of the cone at the lowest possible point.
b) Bend the wire round, pulling it tight, then twist and take under to the central base of the cone.

Wiring a large cone

a) Take two medium-gauge wires and thread each halfway round the circumference of the scales.
b) Twist the wires together at each side and bring them down under the base of the cone.

Wiring walnuts

Walnuts have a soft spot in their base. Take a wire and simply push it through the soft spot into the centre of the nut. Add a drop of glue for extra security, if desired.

Drying and wiring fruit slices

a) Choose fruits that have a firm flesh and few, or no, pips. Slice as thinly as possible. Place on kitchen towelling on a baking tray and cook in a slow oven – the bottom of an Aga or kitchen range is ideal – turning occasionally until the slices are firm. They can be varnished with a clear varnish, but this is not necessary if the flesh is firm.

b) To wire single slices or bundles of slices, take a medium-gauge wire through the slice, as close to the pith as possible, bend over and twist as close to the fruit as you can.

Wiring fresh fruits

a) Take a medium or heavy-gauge wire through the fruit and out the far side, about one-third of the way up the fruit. Repeat with a second wire at right-angles to the first. Bring the wires down and twist together.

b) Alternatively, insert wooden or plastic sticks into the fruit. The advantage of not using wire is that you can eat the fruit afterwards.

Hairpins

Hairpins are made by taking a length of florists' wire and bending it in two. Use the gauge of wire suitable for your purpose.

Extending stems (single leg-mount)

Bend a medium-gauge florists' wire so that one end is longer than the other. Place on the stem towards the end and wrap the longer wire around the stem and the shorter end three times. The free ends should be straight and parallel to one another.

Manipulating leaves

There are many ways to manipulate leaves but the method we have used on pages 50 and 87 uses an *Aspidistra* leaf which is manipulated in the following way. Fold the tip of the *Aspidistra* down to the point where the leaf meets the stalk. Angle it to one side. Take the stem and bring it backwards and over so that it can be pushed through the two layers of the folded leaf. To do this the stems need to be reasonably long.

Preserving foliage

Waxing

The beautiful colours of autumn foliage can be retained by dipping the individual leaves in the melted wax of broken candles.

Glycerine

Glycerining is only suitable for foliage, not flowers, as the addition of glycerine causes the colour to change. Prepare your stems for preserving by removing any damaged leaves or those near the bottom of the stem. Cut the stem ends on the slant to allow the easy intake of liquid and place in water in a cool place for several hours so that the plant becomes 'turgid' with water.

- Take a jam jar and fill it about a quarter full with glycerine. Add to it double the amount of very hot water. Stir well so that the glycerine and water form a mixture. If you wish to add colour to your plant material add a few drops of dye in the colour of your choice.
- Place the stem of plant material to be preserved in the jam jar containing the mixture which should rise approximately 8-10 cm (3-4 in) up the stem.
- Place the plant material in a dry area and monitor the progress of the glycerine mixture climbing the stem into the leaves. You will notice some degree of colour change as the mixture moves upwards.
- When ready remove the foliage and rinse it. Allow to dry on a piece of kitchen towel and, if not being displayed immediately, store in a dry place.

Buying autumn flowers

- Check that the under petals of dahlias are crisp and well-formed as these are the first to deteriorate.

- The berries on *Hypericum* should be plump, with bright green calyces. There should be no black berries on the stem as this is a sign of ageing.

- When purchasing or picking lavender (*Lavandula*) to dry the darker blue colour is more striking but less fragrant than its grey counterpart. The stems should be rigid and not limp and the flowers open, not in bud.

- Chinese lanterns *(Physalis)* can be grown easily in the garden. If purchased from a florist you can buy either green or orange. If you want to dry the lanterns choose the orange for bright colour retention.

- *Liatris* flowers from the top of the stem downwards. Always check that the foliage and stem are a fresh green and not a dull green and mushy.

- *Chrysanthemum* leaves show signs of ageing way before the flowers so for freshness check that there are still leaves on the stem with a fresh appearance and that the flowers are not shedding petals when touched.

- If you want rosehips to stay plump place them in a glycerine solution for a couple of days before arranging. Remove if the colour changes and you want to keep their bright colour.

- If you are combining fruit or vegetables with your flowers, do not buy any with brown marks as they will rot more quickly and in turn shorten the life of your flowers.

- The firmer *Hydrangea* heads are to the touch when you buy them the longer they will last. If they have been cut on the older brown woody part of the stem they will last longer.

Caring for your flowers

- Remove the tips from *Gladiolus.* These are often at an awkward angle. Removing them will create a cleaner line and encourage more flowers on the stem to open.

- To revive *Hydrangea* fill a tall bucket or wide basin with water and submerge the entire flower (head and stem) for several hours. Alternatively cut off 5 cm (2 in) from the bottom of the stem, place in hot water for 60 seconds with the head protected by tissue paper and then allow to stand for several hours in a bucket of deep tepid water.

- *Gloriosa* are sold in special bags which cushion them against damage. Leave them in the bag until you are ready to use them.

- Ripening fruit and vegetables give off a gas called ethylene which shortens the life of flowers. Be aware that the flowers in some of the designs will not last as long when combined with vegetables, but remember that the effect is sometimes worth it!

- If you buy gourds you can extend their life by covering them with clear varnish. Be sure to varnish the entire gourd.

- Hang excess statice (*Limonium*) and Chinese lanterns (*Physalis*) upside-down to dry. They will retain their colour and form perfectly. When dried, strong, pure colours retain their brightness, better than pastels and tones.

- Remove the stamens from inside the lily by pulling rather than cutting which leaves a harsh line. Use a tissue to avoid staining your hands.

- To prevent the ends of amaryllis (*Hippeastrum*) stems curling tie a length of wool around the stem close to the end.

Flower index

A selection of flowers available during the Autumn months.

Blue and Purple

Aconitum
(monkshood)
white

Agapanthus
white

Allium
white

Eryngium (sea holly)

Red and Pink

Celosia argentea var.
cristata (cocks
comb)
yellow/orange

Celosia Plumosa
Group
yellow/green

Anigozanthos
(kangaroo paw)
red/orange/yellow

Dahlia
many colours

Key: (F) = foliage   (B) = berries

Eustoma (lisianthus)
pink, white, yellow
and bi-coloured.

Hydrangea
pink, white

Liatris
white

Limonium
white

Viburnum tinus
(B)

Gladiolus
all colours

Leucadendron
'Safari Sunset'

Malus (crabapple)
really red-orange

Phlox
white, mauve

Skimmia
green
(B)

Orange and Yellow

Achillea (yarrow)
red, white

Alstroemeria
(Peruvian lily)
pink, red, white

Dahlia
many colours

Dianthus (carnation)
many colours

White and Cream

Anthurium
many colours

Chrysanthemum
(bloom)
pink, mauve, yellow,
orange

Chamelaucium
(wax flower)
pink

Chrysanthemum
(spray)
many colours

Green

Amaranthus
(cat's tail)
red, brown

Aspidistra
(F)

Brassica (ornamental
cabbage)
purple

Chrysanthemum
(santini)
many colours

Eremurus (foxtail lily)
peach, white

Euphorbia
(sun spurge)

mini *Gerbera*
many colours

Helianthus
(sunflower)

Physalis
(Chinese lanterns)
green

Freesia
many colours

Hypericum
(St John's wort)
green, red, orange,
brown, yellow
(B)

Lilium longiflorum
(lily)
many colours

Rosa 'Vendella'

Symphoricarpos
(snowberry)
pink
(B)

Fagus (beech)
red
(F)

Papaver (poppy
seedhead)

Hypericum
(St John's wort)
brown, ivory, red,
yellow (B)

*Gomphocarpus
physocarpus*
(Bishops balls)

Triticum (wheat)

Glossary

Aluminum wire
A flexible wire that is available in a wide variety of colours and thicknesses. It is soft enough to cut with scissors.

Bullion or boullion wire
A fine decorative wire with a curl or bend to it that gives a fine shimmer to designs.

Decorative wire
Available in many different colours and thickness, this wire is used to add colour and create other decorative effects.

Double sided tape
Adhesive on both sides, this easily obtainable tape is useful for sticking two objects together unobtrusively.

Floral rings
These are available in a variety of diameters with a styrofoam or plastic base. Posy pads with a solid centre are also available.

Florists' fix
An adhesive putty that is purchased on a roll. It must be used on a clean dry surface in order to ensure it will stick firmly.

Florists' tape
This is a strong tape that can be purchased in two widths.
I recommend purchasing the wider tape. It will adhere to wet surfaces including soaked foam.

Frog
A green plastic disc with four prongs that comes in both large and small sizes – ideally used in conjunction with fix to secure foam.

Leafshine
Available in a spray can which gives shine and gloss to leaves. The surface prior to spraying should be clean and dry. Hold can 40 cm (16 in) from the leaf and apply lightly and evenly. Use in an open space with good ventilation.

Lichen

Lichen can often be found in the country, where the air is pure and clean, growing on walls and trees. It can also be purchased in bags from your local floral supplier.

Mossing pins

Known also as German pins, these are used for securing plant material to foam. You can create your own by taking a length of stub wire and bending it in two.

Orchid tubes

Singapore (*Dendrobium*) and *Cymbidium* orchids are supplied to florists in short plastic tubes with a rubber top with a hole for the stem. Your florist may well be happy to let you have these as they are often thrown away. They are also available from craft shops.

Raffia

This may be purchased in a natural tone or in a wide range of dyed colours. Raffia can be looped, made into bows or tied round containers and bunches to give a natural look.

Raffia covered wire

A specialist product available from some garden centres and wholesalers. The wire gives the raffia extra strength.

Sisal

Sisal is a natural material derived from *Agave sisalana* leaves. It comes in a wide range of colours and is a very useful textural filler.

Spray mount

Spray mount or spray glue, allows you to reposition the items as many times as you like. Spray lightly.

Stem tape

This is used to disguise wires that have been added to extend or give support to fresh plant material. It also conserves the water in the stem.

Stub wire

Stub wire is the name given to lengths of wire (as opposed to wire on a reel) used in floristry to extend, support or replace stems. Wires are measured by gauge – the higher the gauge (metric measurement) the thinner and more flexible the wire.

The Judith Blacklock Flower School

The Judith Blacklock Flower School offers intensive, structured courses in all aspects of flower arranging and the business of floristry. In a quiet secluded mews in Knightsbridge, London, Judith and her team of dedicated teachers give professional information and practical learning skills, using the most beautiful flowers and foliage, that are relevant to participants from all over the world.

From basic design through to the most advanced contemporary work there is a course suitable for every level of expertise.

Private, team building and structured group lessons are available on request.

The Judith Blacklock Flower School
4/5 Kinnerton Place South, London SW1X 8EH
Tel. +44 (0)20 7235 6235
school@judithblacklock.com
www.judithblacklock.com

Acknowledgements

Photography

All photographs Tobias Smith except for
Judith Blacklock: pages 13, 15, 25, 51, 73, 75, 85, 101
Lyndon Parker: pages 9, 11, 13, 53, 65, 69, 83, 85, 87

© iStockphoto.com/Gina Luck: page 99

Line Drawings: Tomoko Nakamoto
Botanical Editor: Dr. Christina Curtis
Assistant Editor: Rachel Petty

As always a huge thank you to everyone who helped with the recipes. A special thanks to Rachel Petty and to my invaluable assistant Chicka Yoshida who is now living in Singapore. I would also like to mention Thomasz Koson and the team at the school. I also received wonderful support from Gail Bearman, Darren Black, Claire Bond, Betsy Carrier, Pat Dibben, Mo Duffill, Dawn Jennings, Ann Marie Kendrick, Katherine Scott and my mother Joan Ward who is my inspiration and who allowed me to photograph at her home in Cumbria.

The photographers Toby and Lyndon, Amanda Hawkes, Christina Curtis and Tomoko Nakamoto have been a wonderful team with which to work.